An Absolute
Relationship
to Life

An Absolute Relationship to Life

A Talk on Enlightenment and the Human Condition

ANDREW COHEN

MOKSHA PRESS 1997

Moksha Press Cataloging
Cohen, Andrew, 1955 Oct. 23-
An absolute relationship to life: a talk on enlightenment
and the human condition / Andrew Cohen.
p. cm.
ISBN 1-883929-19-9
1. Life.   2. Self.   I. Title.
BD431   1997
128—dc21

Preface

I began teaching in 1986 and in the over ten years that have passed since that time, I have learned something very important. Spiritual experiences, as profound as they may appear to be, usually do not in and of themselves lastingly enlighten. Nor do they, it seems in most cases, deeply transform the individual's relationship to the three most confusing aspects of the human experience: the movement of time, the presence of thought and the arising of feeling. Indeed, the movement of time, the presence of thought and the arising of feeling, for all but a very few, seem to instantly obscure the awareness of an absolute depth without which the direct perception of the true and right relationship of all things is impossible.

It has become very clear to me that it is the one-pointed *contemplation* of our actual relationship to these most fundamental aspects of our experience, rather than brief interludes of nondual perception, that in the long run creates the powerful foundation upon which discriminating wisdom—the wisdom that liberates—can become manifest.

This talk was given without premeditation in Amsterdam, Holland on July 10, 1996 and was edited for clarity the following December.

Foreword

"Could I speak with John Wren-Lewis?" asked the unfamiliar American voice on the other end of the line one day in 1990, adding, "This is Andrew Cohen calling from California." I was taken aback. Yes, I knew the name, having written to him from my Sydney home some weeks earlier, on the recommendation of a British academic who'd compiled a directory of modern western spiritual teachers. But I knew nothing about Andrew beyond my friend's assurance that he was one of the few who might be approachable person-to-person, rather than as an exalted Master open only to guru-disciple relationships. The very most I'd expected in reply was a letter, but here on the line from America was the man himself, explaining that he'd been away in India until now—and he proceeded to ask all kinds of searching questions about my letter. I was impressed that here indeed was a spiritual teacher with a difference.

Our friendship has grown steadily ever since, and writing this foreword in a way brings it full circle. For my need in approaching Andrew back then arose from having been catapulted willy-nilly, just a few years before, into precisely the "absolute relationship to life" which is the subject of this book. I hadn't been following any spiritual path or seeking any kind of enlightenment, for as a scientist I'd regarded the whole idea of mystical consciousness as meaningless mystification. But in 1983 I was accidently brought to the point of death by poisoning, and came back from the brink—a total stop in time, thought and feeling—with an entirely new sense of identity.

Formerly I'd seen myself and everyone else as separate persons, each of us using thought to preserve and improve life along the line of time, continually evaluating the outcome by our good or bad feelings. Now, by total contrast, I was experiencing myself as Undivided Life moving *into* time, with thoughts and feelings simply transient eddies in a wonderful impersonal life-flow. In fact I'd had thrust upon me the very changes which Andrew spells out in this book as necessary elements of true freedom. I found exactly what he emphasizes here—that the changed identity was in no way a move "out of this world." On the contrary, it gave me a freedom for living *in* this world which I'd never before imagined possible. But I also found that adjusting to such freedom continually raises problems which only folk with firsthand knowledge of absolute relationship to life could begin to appreciate.

So I can now confirm from my own direct experience the accuracy and importance of the spiritual life-mode which Andrew delineates in the pages that follow. He highlights the radical moment-by-moment, day-by-day revolution against common human attitudes to time, thought and feeling which the members of any serious spiritual community must discover and maintain in their relationships to each other and the world. In fact he translates into everyday practicalities what T.S. Eliot, at the climax of his great spiritual poem *Little Gidding*, called

> A condition of complete simplicity
> Costing not less than everything.

And a revolutionary message is here given a revolutionary medium by the Moksha Press. In presenting this and other special talks by Andrew as pocket-sized books that can be read within the hour, they have revived a format which the vicissitudes of publishing economics have made very rare in recent decades, yet in the past has played a vital part in revolutions, social and spiritual alike. I am delighted to be contributing a foreword to a Tract for the Times.

John Wren-Lewis
Honorary Associate
School of Studies in Religion
University of Sydney

Introduction

Very few people think deeply about life. And of those who do, even fewer think deeply about what it means to be a human being in relationship to that which is beyond measure, that which is Absolute.

What does it mean to have a relationship to life that is absolute? Through asking ourselves this simple question everything can be revealed.

Over the years that I have been teaching, it has become apparent to me that most people do not have an Absolute Relationship to Life. In fact, it seems for most of us even the notion of a relationship to life that is absolute appears overwhelming in its implications. But for those of us who are sincerely interested in liberating ourselves from fear, ignorance and self-deception, contemplation of the profound implications of a relationship to life, to all human experience, that is absolute is imperative. Because without a clear understanding of what an Absolute Relationship to Life actually is, the possibility of any genuine victory over fear, ignorance and self-deception will remain only an idea in the mind.

In order to understand what an Absolute Relationship to Life is, I'm going to speak about some of the fundamental components of the enlightened perspective. I'm going to speak about a way of relating to our own experience from the enlightened perspective rather than a perspective that is based upon ignorance and unenlightenment.

The question that I want to go into is: What does it

mean to have an Absolute Relationship to Life? What does it mean to have an absolute relationship to the human experience?

Part 1

An
Absolute
Relationship
to
Time

There are three fundamental components of the enlightened perspective that are essential to look into in order to be able to find out what an Absolute Relationship to Life actually is. The first is our relationship to time and the movement of time.

An absolute relationship to time and the movement of time from the enlightened perspective means that we have *stopped waiting*.

Because our relationship to time and the movement of time is not absolute, without being aware of it, most of us spend almost our entire lives trapped in a process of endlessly waiting. An absolute relationship to time means that we have stopped waiting in a way that is absolute in relationship to the entire experience of being alive.

Now if we can recognize that we spend almost our entire lives trapped in the process of waiting, it becomes obvious that if it was possible to stop waiting in a way that was absolute—absolute means complete, without conditions—then *everything* would change. You see, if we are always waiting in our fundamental relationship to life, then our relationship to time and the movement of time will *have* to be one of limitation. When we are trapped by the process of waiting in our fundamental relationship to being alive, we will be living in a constant state of anticipation of what is yet to come.

Why do we do this? Because we hope that in the future the experience of being alive will get better. It's that simple. We live in the constant hope that things will improve in the future. Now obviously if we are constantly trapped in this process of waiting for things to change, to get better, it will be impossible for us to experience what it means to be fully alive NOW.

When our relationship to time and the movement of time is not absolute, no matter what occurs and no matter what we experience, positive or negative, pleasant or unpleasant, *we will continue to wait*. When we are lucky enough to experience true happiness, even then we will continue to wait. Why? Because without realizing it, we are already anticipating its demise. In the very same way, when we experience intense fear or troubling doubt, we will not be able to be fully present, fully alive, because we will still be trapped in the process of waiting—waiting for that experience to go away.

If we look very closely, we can see that this matter of constantly waiting in relationship to time and the movement of time is, on an emotional and psychological level, simply a withholding of ourselves. A fundamental holding back in relationship to the experience of life. We are waiting to let go, we are waiting for things to change, we are waiting to be able to fully give ourselves, but in the meantime we are still waiting. This is why we find that so few of us seem to be fully alive. This is why so few of us seem to be *truly* present.

If we are constantly waiting in relationship to time and the movement of time, we will be living in a state of almost unending distraction—unending distraction because we are living in constant anticipation of what is to come. This is a state of bondage.

When we experience spiritual insight, we recognize that the reason that we suffer, that our fundamental experience of life is one of limitation, is not because there is something wonderful that we have not yet experienced. It is only because without realizing it we have chosen to wait. When we deeply realize this for ourselves, we simply cease to wait. In that alone everything changes.

An absolute relationship to time is one in which we have stopped waiting in a way that is absolute. That means we have stopped waiting for anything fundamental to occur in order to be.

Part 2

An
Absolute
Relationship
to
Thought

*W*hat is a relationship to thought and the movement of thought that is absolute? The second component of the enlightened perspective is our relationship to thought. Many great spiritual teachers of the past and present have said that our fundamental predicament can be found by scrutinizing our relationship to thought. We hear this over and over again. So from the perspective of an Absolute Relationship to Life, what is an absolute relationship to thought and the movement of thought?

Any human being who has done even a little bit of introspection will have recognized for themselves that they spend the majority of their time lost in and busy with thought and the movement of thought. We might even say *compulsively* busy with thought and the movement of thought. Indeed, there seem to be very few moments in life when we find ourselves pleasantly free from and undistracted by the movement of thought. And those moments when we recognize ourselves to be undistracted by thought are almost always times of intense happiness, profound joy, and most important of all, deep peace. In fact, it seems that it is not possible for us to experience deep peace when we are busy with thought and the movement of thought.

A relationship to thought that is absolute is a relationship to thought that is free, that is liberated. *A relationship to thought that is absolute is one in which the individual has no doubt whatsoever that thought is only thought.* It's very simple.

Understand that everything that I'm speaking about here is *deceptively* simple. Please don't be fooled by that. It's one thing to declare that an absolute relationship to thought is one in which thought is recognized to be only thought. Theoretically this is very simple, but the practical implications of recognizing that thought is only thought and *nothing but thought* are enormous. The fact is, in the privacy of our own inner world, most of us have a very hard time believing that thought *is* only thought.

What does it actually mean when I say that thought is only thought? It means that *thought is not self*. This is the most fundamental spiritual insight—that thought is *not* self, that thought is *only* thought. You see, without recognizing this, we blindly presume that thought and the movement of thought is actually the self, the *personal* self.

For example, while walking down the street we may unexpectedly find ourselves thinking a virtuous thought, and as a result believe ourselves to be a "good" person. A few minutes later, we may find to our dismay, nasty, mean and malicious thoughts moving inside our head, and as a result then believe ourselves to be a "bad" person. This kind of confusion occurs all the time, for without realizing it, over and over and over again we believe that *what we think is who we are*.

An absolute relationship to thought means that the individual has discovered that thought in and of itself is only thought and *has no self nature*. What does that mean? It means that the mere presence of thought has no significance whatsoever except that which we *choose* to give it.

So once again, an absolute relationship to thought is one in which the individual has recognized for themselves beyond any doubt that thought in and of itself has no significance whatsoever, except that which we choose to give it. THIS IS VERY IMPORTANT. Because most people do not have an absolute relationship to thought and the movement of thought, they live almost their entire lives distracted by the movement of what are only shadows, believing them to be real entities that have tremendous power and great significance. It is because of this that they rarely experience intense happiness, profound joy or deep peace.

Part 3

An
Absolute
Relationship
to
Feeling

The third component of the enlightened perspective is our relationship to the experience of feeling. Looking into the question of what an Absolute Relationship to Life is, we have to ask: What is an absolute relationship to the experience of feeling?

When speaking about the experience of feeling, I'm referring to our relationship to happiness and pleasure on one hand, and our relationship to fear and insecurity on the other. What is an absolute relationship to the experience of happiness, to pleasurable feelings? And what is an absolute relationship to feelings that are challenging and difficult, to fear and insecurity?

If we look closely at the human experience we will find that fundamentally we live to experience as much pleasure as we can, while simultaneously we try to avoid experiencing as much fear and insecurity as possible. This is understandable. Who wouldn't want to feel good and who would want to feel bad?

With close scrutiny, we find that the perspective that we have upon our own experience, and therefore upon the whole experience of being alive, seems to be dominated in a fundamental way by the movement of feeling. When we feel happy, the experience of life appears to be a good thing. So much seems to be possible when we are happy. If we are *really* happy, we may even believe that it's possible to be free in this life. In the presence of profound happiness, it seems that anything is possible. But when that feeling is absent, or even worse when we feel terrible, when we find ourselves in the midst of tremendous fear and insecurity, we won't even want to hear about the possibility of liberation.

A relationship to the movement of feeling that is not absolute is one where our relationship to our experience is constantly changing because of the way we feel. Indeed, it is illuminating to discover the degree to which our perspective shifts and moves in relationship to how we feel in any particular moment.

For example, when we experience joy, there is much more room within us for others, but when we experience unpleasant feelings, we find it very difficult to feel concern for anyone other than our own self. Over the years that I have been teaching, I have noticed that often when people would begin to experience joy or bliss their perspective would automatically become very vast. As a result they would declare, "Oh my goodness, I'm not the only one who exists!" And then I would notice that the instant that same individual would experience fear or confusion, their newly expanded perspective usually would disappear. Suddenly all they seemed to be aware of was the fact that they didn't feel good and appeared to be at a loss to see beyond it.

It is precisely this loss of perspective that causes so many of us to be untrustworthy. Unwittingly, we constantly allow ourselves to be dominated by how we feel. We allow our perspective, and therefore our relationship to the entire experience of being alive, to be ruled by our emotional experience. It is fascinating to see how the expression of the personality endlessly shifts and changes in subtle ways simply because of the presence of different emotions.

An absolute relationship to the experience of feeling is one in which the personality expresses ONE relationship to life—one perspective, one self. And the expression of that one self is no longer dependent upon the presence of any particular feeling. Indeed, an absolute relationship to the experience of feeling is liberation from emotional slavery, liberation from the almost unending tyranny that most of us, without being fully aware of it, are imprisoned by.

An absolute relationship to the experience of feeling becomes possible when the individual discovers for themselves that the presence of any particular feeling does not necessarily have to mean anything at all about the experiencer. That would mean that our perspective upon our experience was no longer dominated by the movement of particular feelings. Therefore, whether we were experiencing great happiness and joy, or fear and confusion, a fundamental perspective in relationship to all of our experience would be unshakable.

Part 4

An
Absolute
Relationship
to
Life

*I*t's very important to ask the question *"What is an Absolute Relationship to Life?"* in the biggest possible way. In our search for freedom, too easily we can become preoccupied with only our relationship to time, or only our relationship to thought, or only our relationship to feeling. In so doing we miss the biggest possible perspective. The biggest possible perspective has to include all three.

Once again, in our relationship to the experience of time, we have to ask ourselves: Am I waiting? Am I *always* waiting? Is the very fact that I'm waiting making it impossible for me to experience what it means to be fully alive? If the answer is yes, then would we stop waiting? Would we have the courage to take the overwhelming risk of ceasing to wait? If we would, we would discover a degree of vulnerability that is excruciating even to consider, let alone directly experience for ourselves. When we truly cease to wait, we will have no future left—which means *this is it*. There's no longer any time to prepare, no second chance. That's what it means. When we stop waiting we no longer hold back—we give *everything*. When we give everything, we'll have nothing left. And that's the whole point—*if* we want to be free.

In our relationship to thought, if it's true that thought is only thought, that thought is not self, *then we have to have the courage to take it seriously*. Suddenly the question of who we actually are begs to be answered. Who am I, who believed himself or herself to be this thought or that thought? Who am I, who has now realized that I am not anything that I think, that I never have been and never could be? *Who am I?*

Following this inquiry to the end forces an ungraspable mystery to reveal itself, and one *has* to be ready to come to terms with it if one is sincere. You see when we truly, not just merely intellectually but directly and experientially, recognize that we are not thought and the movement of thought, then we discover space, *infinite space*. And in the end, it is the direct experiential discovery of that infinite space that reveals our potential to be free from thought and the movement of thought. It is this discovery that has the power to release us from the compulsive and hypnotic belief that thought is self.

In our relationship to feeling, most of us are enslaved to a degree that is terrifying to consider. We are so easily confused by the presence of fear. And in the confusion that the presence of fear generates, we lose our equilibrium, suddenly finding it difficult to remember what's true or what's false. Too often, without being aware of it, we are willing to sell our souls in order to experience only a few moments of relief. We are so ready to compromise simply to escape. This is the misery of our condition. This is the tragic state that most of us find ourselves in.

What would it be like to no longer be a slave to the experience of feeling? If we were no longer a slave to the experience of feeling, in the face of fear we would not be moved. If we were no longer a slave to the experience of feeling, *even when we experienced ecstasy we would not waver*.

If we want to be free, our relationship to time, our relationship to thought and our relationship to feeling is EVERYTHING—the difference between heaven and hell, freedom and bondage. Through looking into this question alone—What is an Absolute Relationship to Life?—everything that we could possibly need to know to be a liberated human being can be found.

Andrew Cohen is not just a spiritual teacher—he is an inspiring phenomenon. Since his awakening in 1986 he has only lived, breathed and spoken of one thing: the potential of total liberation from the bondage of ignorance, superstition and selfishness. Powerless to limit his unceasing investigation, he has looked at the "jewel of enlightenment" from every angle, and given birth to a teaching that is vast and subtle, yet incomparably direct and revolutionary in its impact.

Through his public teachings, his books and his meetings with spiritual leaders of almost every tradition, he has tirelessly sought to convey his discovery that spiritual liberation's true significance is its potential to completely transform not only the individual, but the entire way that human beings, as *a race, live together. In sharp contrast to the cynicism which is so pervasive today, yet with full awareness of the difficult challenges that we face, he has dared to teach and to show that it is indeed possible to bring heaven to earth. This powerful message of unity, openness and love has inspired many who have heard it to join together to prove its reality with their own lives, igniting an ever-expanding international revolution of tremendous vitality and significance.*

BOOKS BY ANDREW COHEN

Freedom Has No History

The Challenge of Enlightenment

An Unconditional Relationship to Life

Enlightenment Is a Secret

Autobiography of an Awakening

My Master Is My Self

For more information about Andrew Cohen and his teaching please contact:

Moksha Foundation - *a nonprofit organization founded in 1988 to support and facilitate the teaching work of Andrew Cohen. It is dedicated to the enlightenment of the individual and the expression of enlightenment in the world.*

FACE - *Friends of Andrew Cohen Everywhere represents the larger body of Andrew Cohen's students who have come together to try to manifest sanity in an insane world.*

North America

MOKSHA FOUNDATION and
INTERNATIONAL CENTER FOR FACE
P.O. Box 2360
Lenox, MA 01240 USA
tel: 413-637-6000 or 800-376-3210
fax: 413-637-6015
email: moksha@moksha.org
website: http://www.moksha.org

FACE BOSTON
2269 Massachusetts Avenue
Cambridge, MA 02140 USA
tel: 617-492-2848
fax: 617-876-3525
email: 73214.602@compuserve.com

FACE TORONTO
167 Spadina Road
Toronto, Ontario, Canada M5R 2T9
tel: 416-944-8175
fax: 416-964-8137
email: 104361.536@compuserve.com

FACE NEW YORK
tel: 212-978-4275
email: info@faceny.org

Europe

FACE LONDON
Centre Studios
Englands Lane
London NW3 4YD UK
tel: 44-171-483-3732
fax: 44-171-916-3170
email: 100074.3662@compuserve.com
website: http://www.moksha.org/faceag.htm

FACE AMSTERDAM
Sarphatistraat 70
1018 GR Amsterdam, Holland
tel: 31-20-639-2501
fax: 31-20-639-1417
email: 100412.160@compuserve.com
website: http://www.moksha.org/face/nl

FACE COLOGNE
Elsassstrasse 69
50677 Cologne, Germany
tel: 49-221-310-1040
fax: 49-221-331-9439
email: 100660.1375@compuserve.com

Other Centers

FACE TEL AVIV
8 Remez Street
Tel Aviv, Israel 62096
tel: 972-3695-3697
fax: 972-3691-6828
email: 100274.3277@compuserve.com

FACE SYDNEY
479 Darling Street
Balmain, Sydney
NSW 2041 Australia
tel/fax: 61-2-9555-2932
email: 105312.2467@compuserve.com